My name is Tony Ciampa and this book is full of poems about the emotions that result from the life and times of me and my friends. Most of the poems have four short parts, so I creatively called them four part poems, then put a hashtag in front.

I've been publishing these poems on Instagram for quite some time now, and it's been really inspiring to see so many of you relate to my words. Because of this, I decided to make an interactive book so we could all share our words together.

The way it works is pretty simple.

To start, please visit my Instagram, @emolabs, for some visual examples of how I present my poems. Hopefully you'll be encouraged to do the same, so the bulk of the book is pages worth of my poems for you to take out into your daily life, photograph and share on Instagram.

In keeping with the spirit of community, it would be awesome if you'd use the tag "#fourpartpoems." If you want to take it even further, tag someone: a friend, a lover, a former lover. Anyone. Be bold, great things may come of it. Terrible things may come of it too, but terrible things make for great stories you can someday tell to your grandchildren as they bounce up and down on your lap.

The last part of the book, as you may have noticed, is blank pages. Please, if there's something you need to get off your chest, for better or worse, grab a pen and add your verse to the story.

I can't wait to see what you come up with.

One final note:

This book is meant to be destroyed. Cross out the words, write new ones, tear out the pages and mail them to someone who needs to hear them.

Take this book with you wherever you go and ruin it in the most beautiful way you know how.

And now, let's get started.

→

i'd hoped i'd see you in the morning

with the sun upon your face

but you were only mine for one night

you had other boys to chase

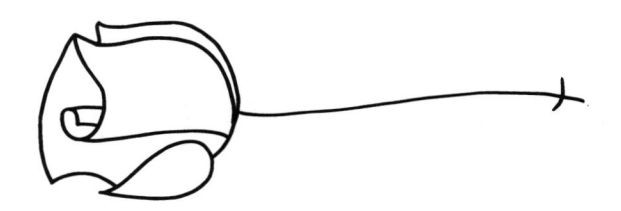

my bed's not always empty
but the mornings feel that way

when you're gone before i wake up

and i'm glad you didn't stay

⟶

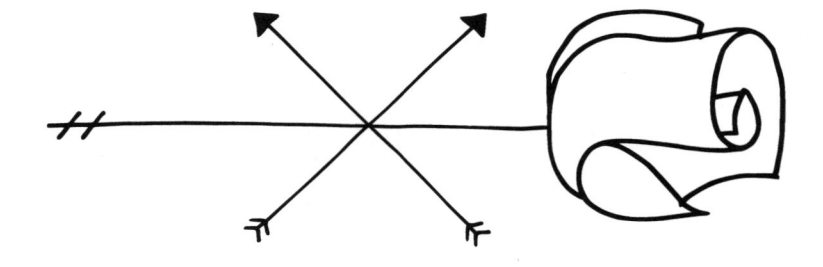

the first week brought a romance

that we thought would never fade

but the second brought reality

it looks like you got afraid

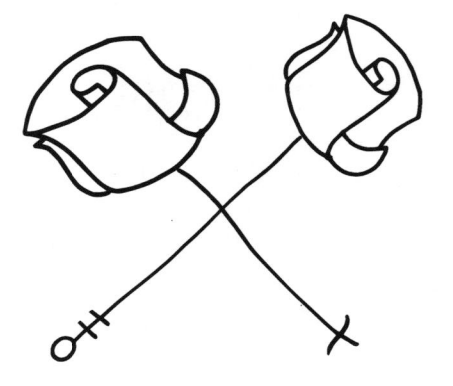

⟶

this may just be for one night

i don't care that we just met

we can still play love 'til morning

truth or dare the sun to set

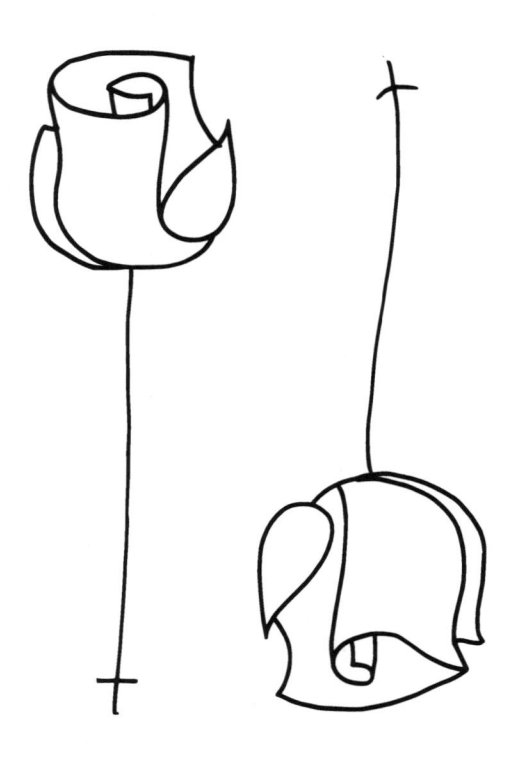

when the northeast winters
shook my bones

i had your hand to hold

now it's springtime in the south

and i've never felt so cold

i've never bared a loss

that i couldn't drink away

but my liver needs a break

so i'm hoping that you'll stay

⟶

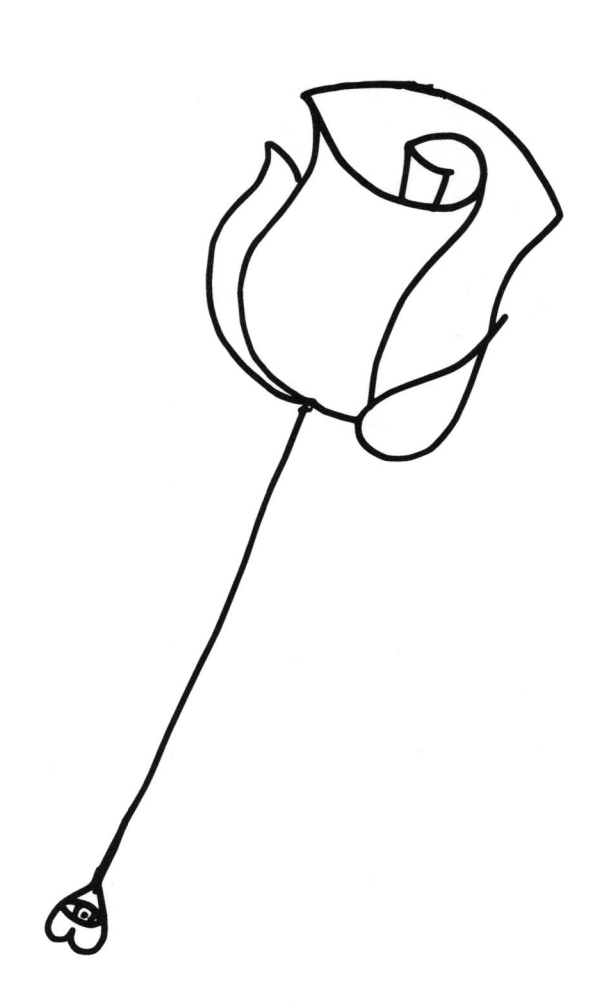

⟶

the grass probably won't be greener

no matter where i roam

because if you're not by my side

than i could never call it home

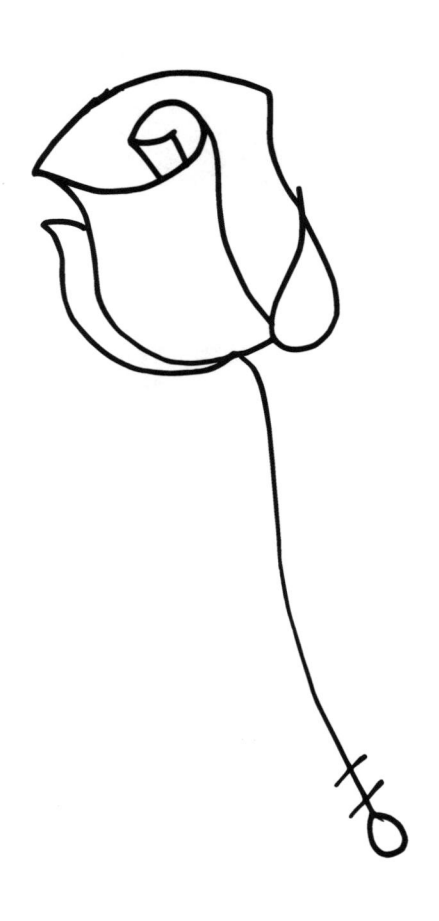

this night will surely end
and we'll go our separate ways

for lust can thrive in darkness

but true love requires days

→

at night we hear the trains

and i feel as your heart races

it feels like i sleep alone

when you dream of other places

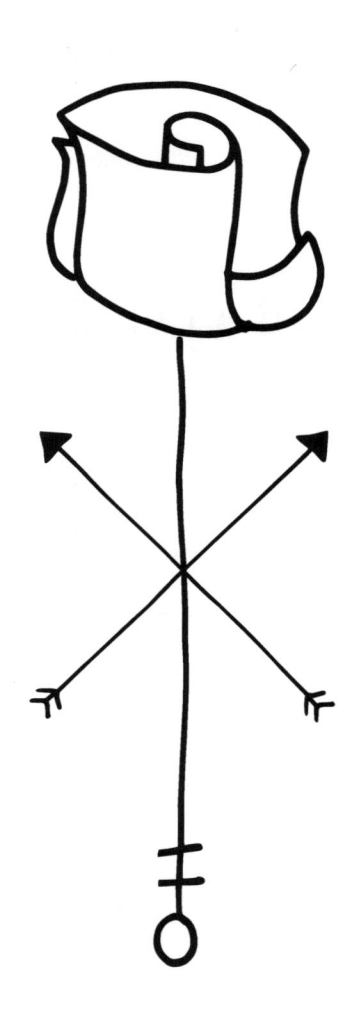

i hate the way your eyes get

when you're driving late at night

because i know you dream of running

and i fear that soon you might

i always talk about progression

but it's coming pretty slow

for i still listen to the upsides

the way i did three years ago

and i still drink myself to sleep

to these same old fucking songs

so if moving forward's right

then i guess i'm living wrong

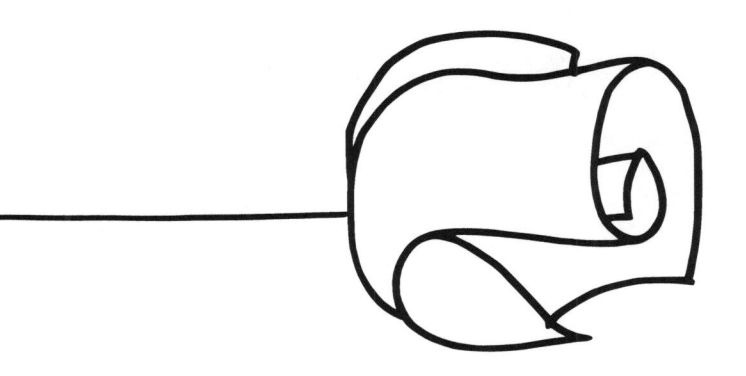

when i left i thought i'd bury

all these memories we had

but now my very favorite ones

only serve to make me sad

»⎯⎯⎯→

and every door where i live now

is one i know you won't walk through

so i'll stay pissed at every sunset

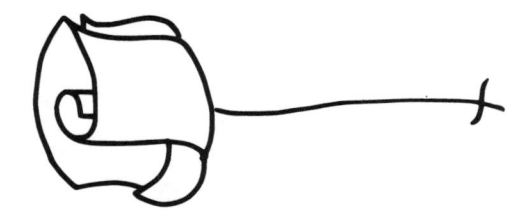

not as beautiful as you

⟶

my mind is plagued by these
old memories

of friends i no longer see

and i can't seem to relive them

i'll admit that it kills me

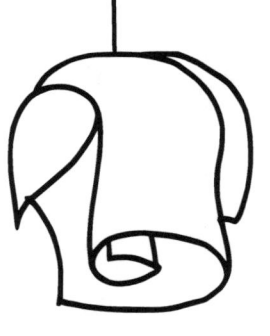

→

so i dream of moving home

where i'll try to relive the past

but when i said let's live like kids

you said that nothing good can last

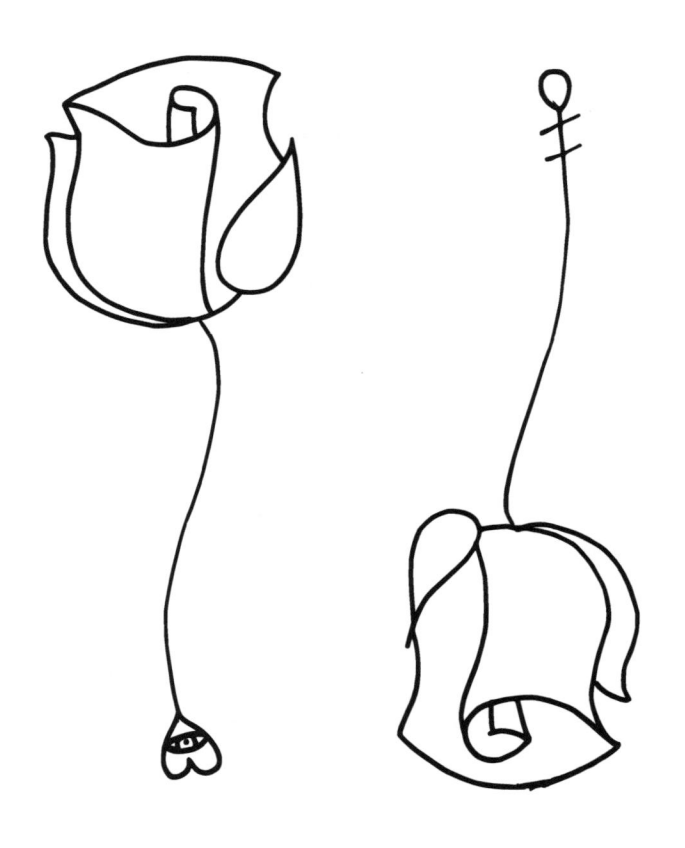

i'll always be grateful
whether you choose to stay or leave

you made my heart more than a muscle

that just beats to help me breathe

⟶

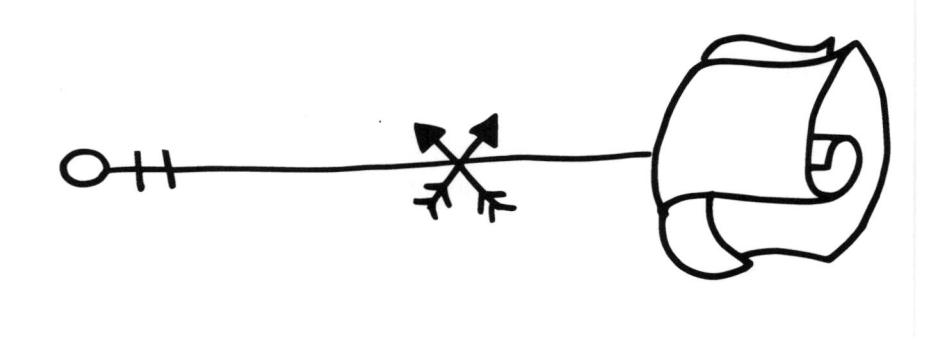

we woke and said good morning

but should've probably said good night

because the morning's a beginning

and we see our end in sight

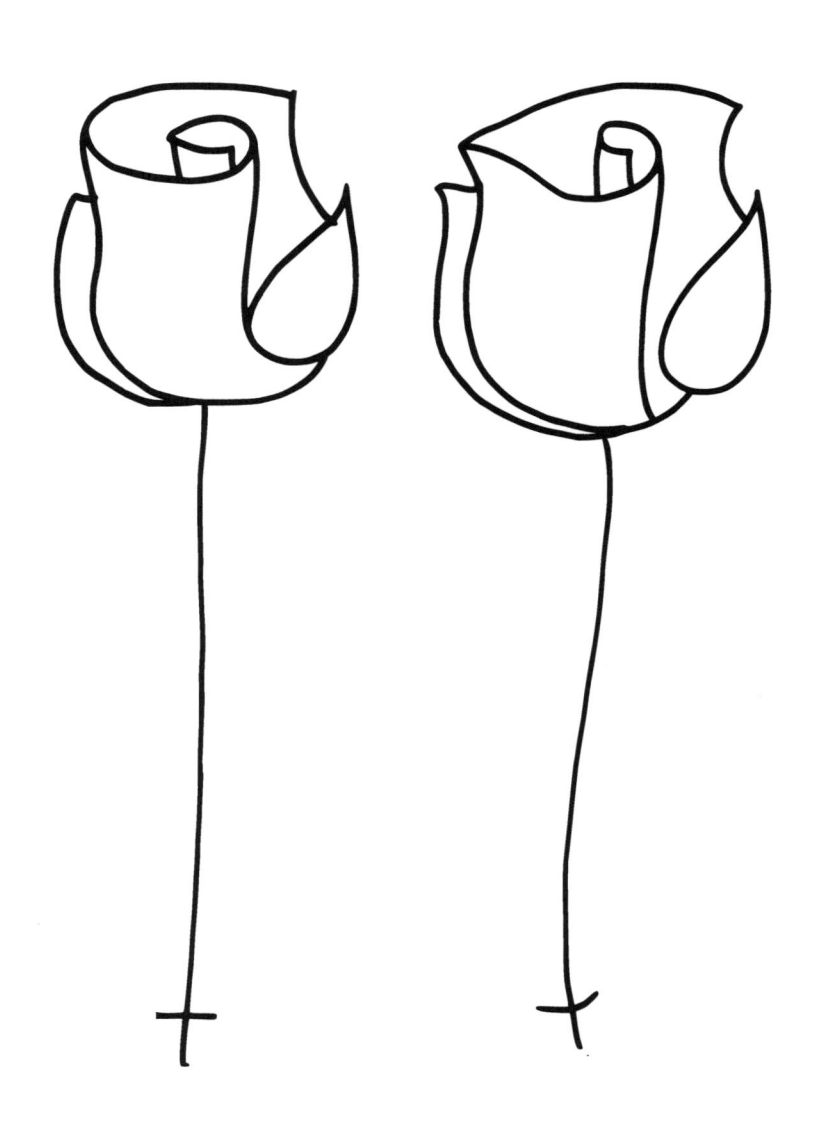

i wasn't that fond of my own name

until i heard it from your lips

not content with my own fingers

until they slid across your hips

→

i traveled the world

tried to hold every hand

and slept in more beds

than i'd planned

but i'm restless again

so i've learned there's a cost

when you mix love and lust

you get lost

→

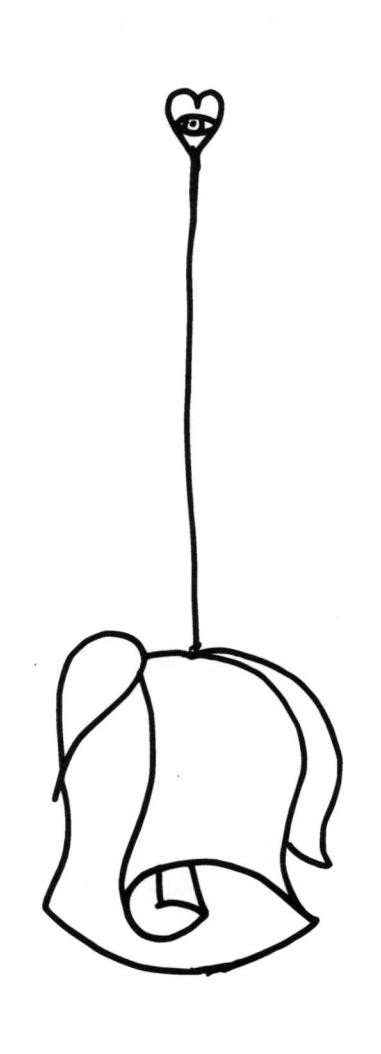

i could burn all of your photos

and set fire to our bed

but how much good could that do

when you live inside my head

i hope some days you feel alive

i hope you live for sleepless nights

i hope you fall in love

and it cures your fear of heights

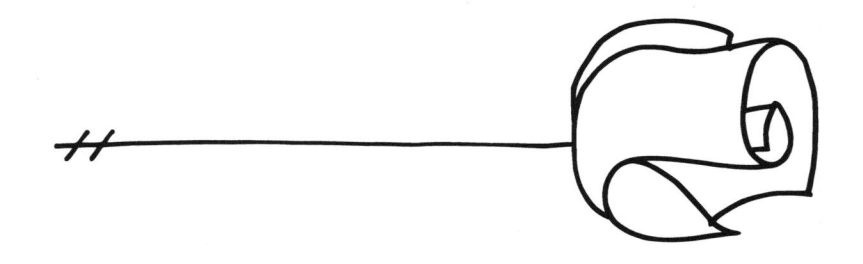

→

and i hope somebody treats you right

and spends sleepless nights with you

i hope he climbs a mountain

to prove you're still his favorite view

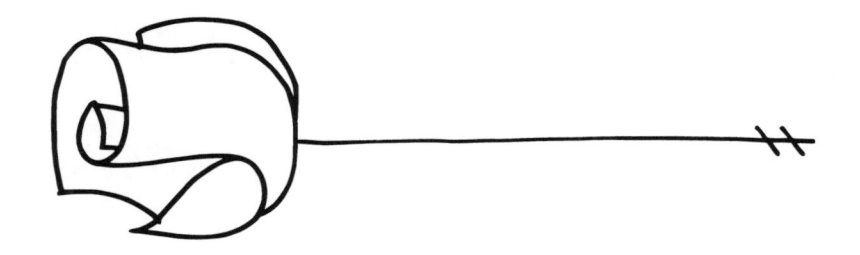

here's to perfect summer nights

in your favorite floral dress

with your fingers wrapped in mine

and your hair a breezy mess

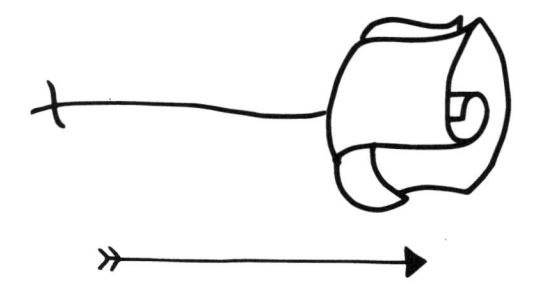

see i've been picking off your petals

and it feels a lot like love

how we share all of these moments

that i feel unworthy of

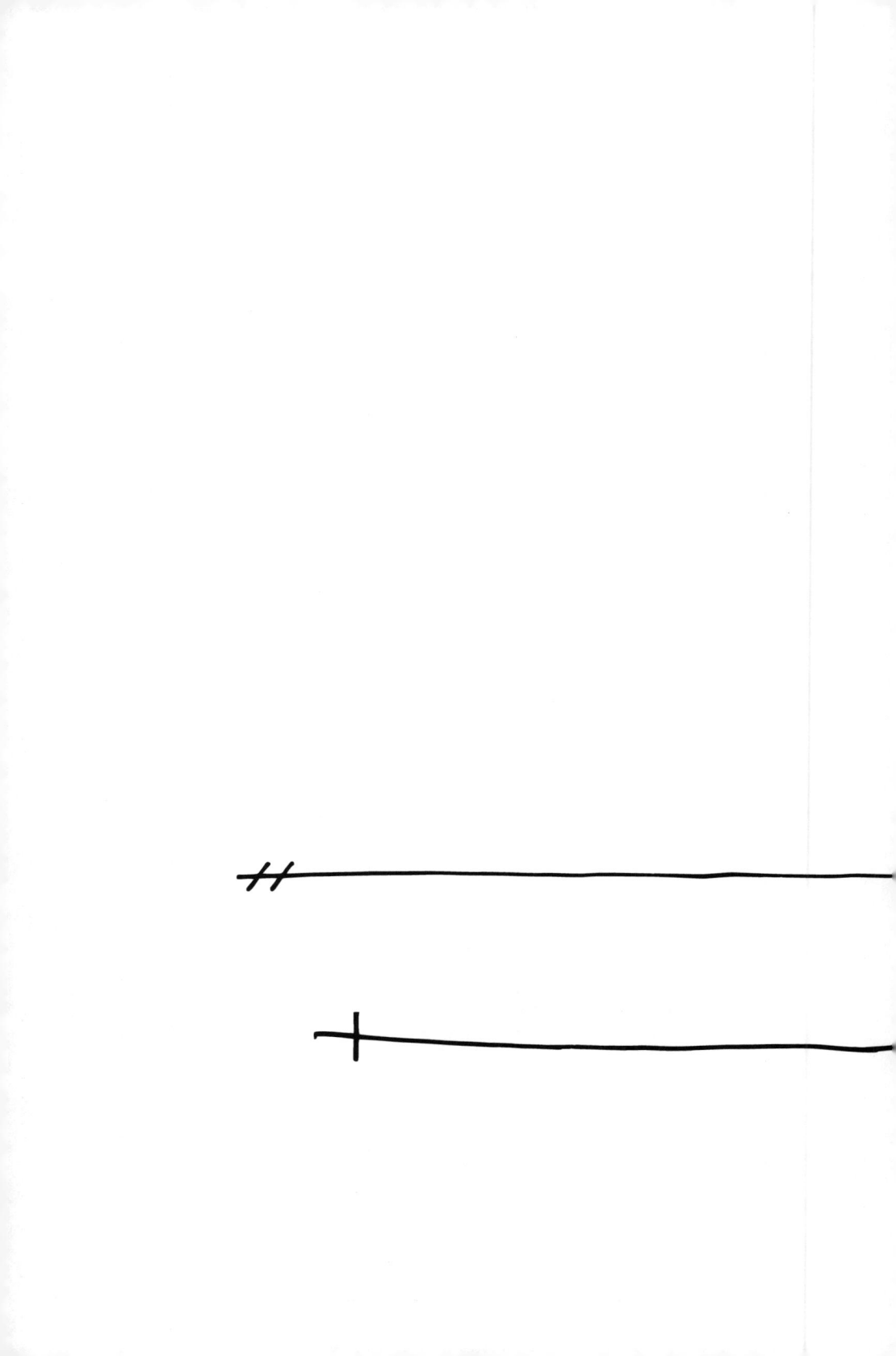

you cover up your scars
so that nobody can look

but your scars contain your story
and i want to read your book

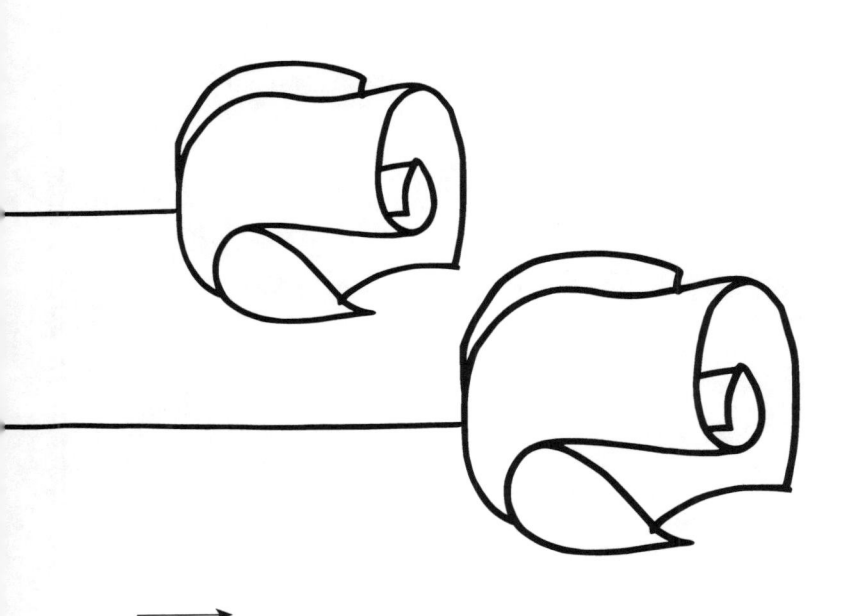

→

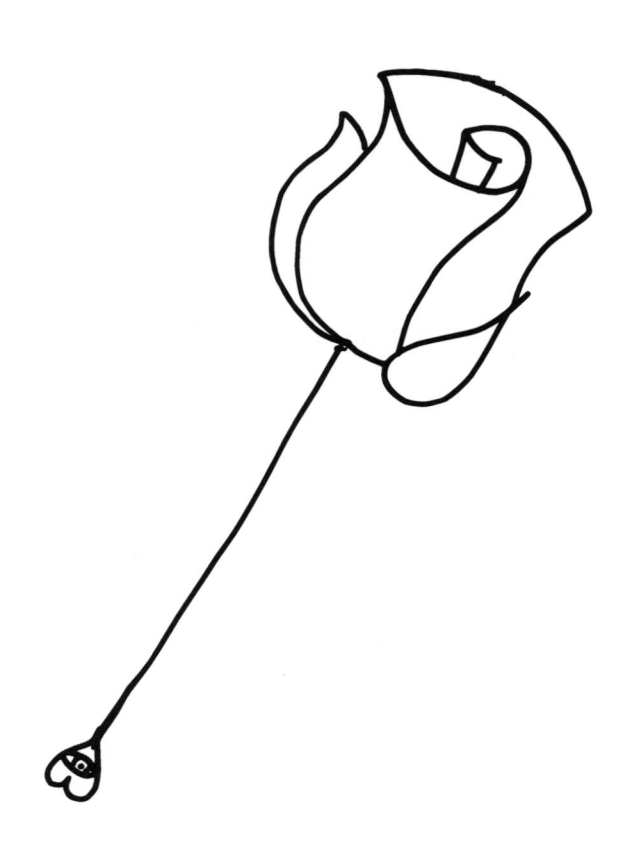

→

you were all the beauty i had eyes for

from the first day that we met

but you've gone and left a void

i'll try to fill with each sunset

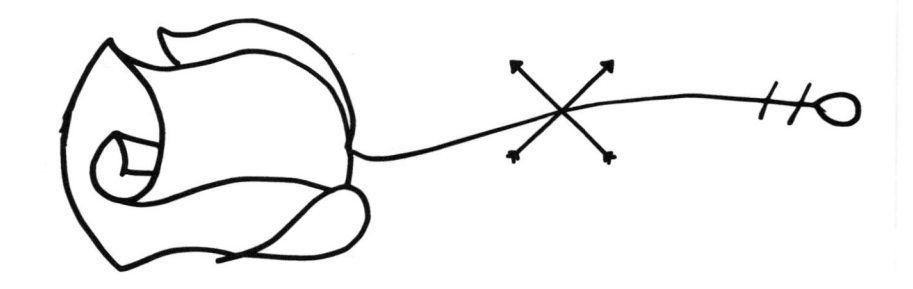

you're always driving way too fast

and you smoke a pack a day

so what makes love so big a risk

that you had to run away

we're 1,000 miles away
but the nights still feel like ours

when we stare up at the sky
and know we're seeing the same stars

so on cloudy nights like these
i don't know how i'll make it through

i hope that i can fall asleep
at least then i can dream of you

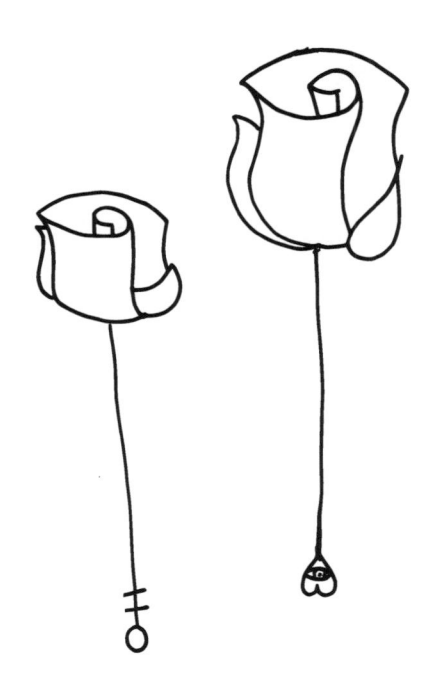

⟶

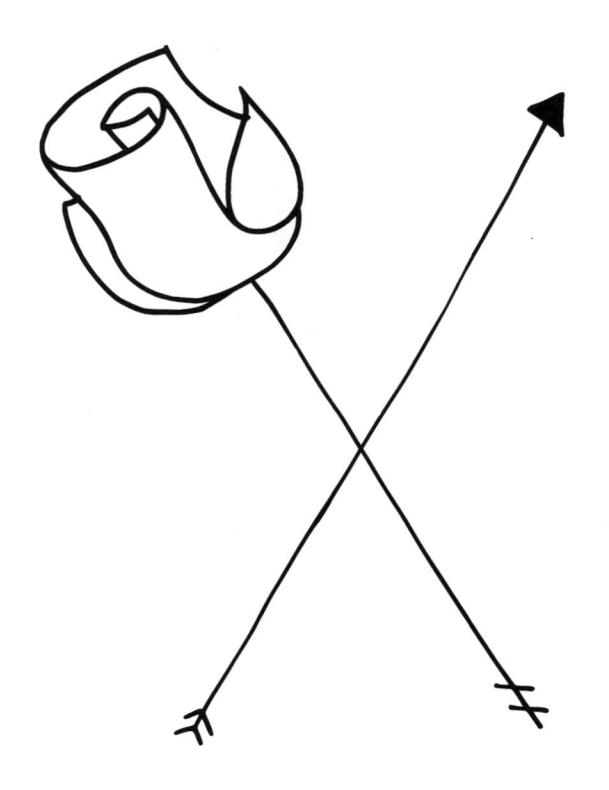

i can't say i won't miss you

but i hope your tears have dried

because heartbreak is not knowing

and we'll always know we tried

→

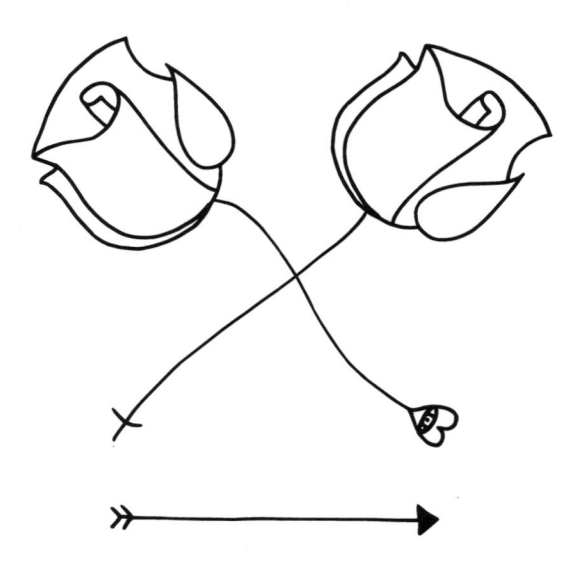

i'm content to wander

if your hand is wrapped in mine

because if we're lost together

then we have nothing left to find

→

let's go find a place together

you and i can call our own

because the world is full of beauty

that i'd hate to see alone

our old house is all but empty

still i walk by every day

to slip a letter in the door

of things i'll never get to say

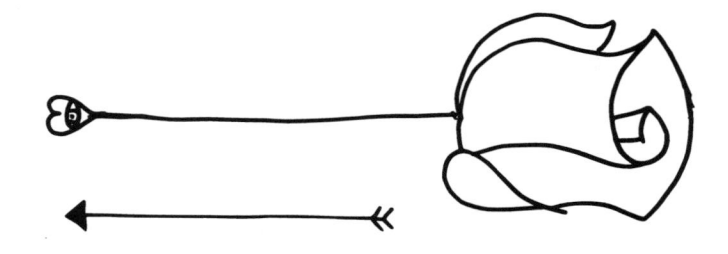

they remind you that i miss you

while i'm living out our years

i pretend your ghost can read them

and the dust is just your tears

→

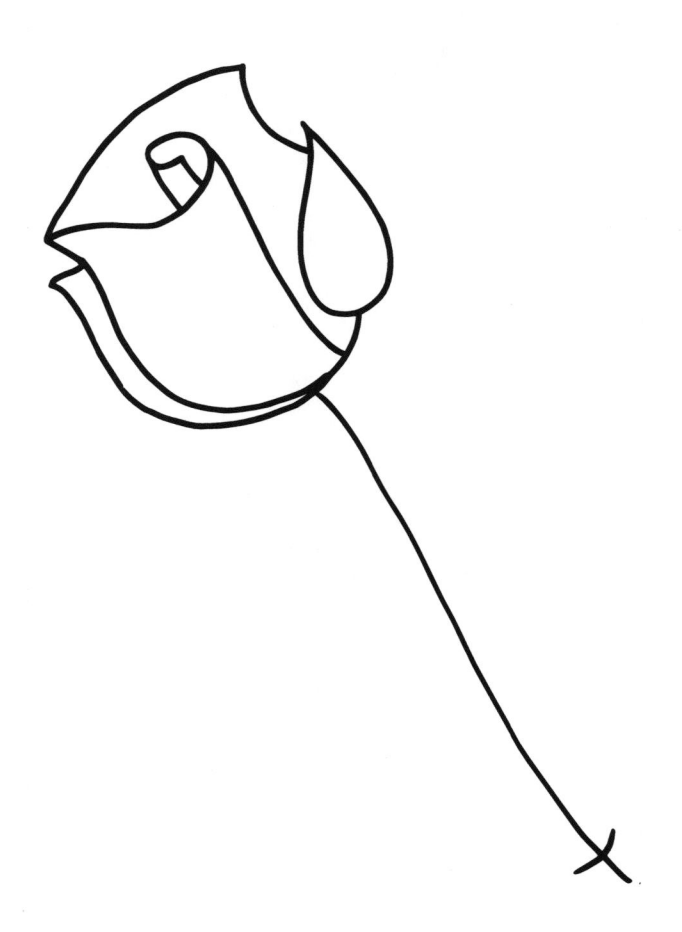

→

every night i rush to bed

and get to counting all my sheep

because my pillow's lost your scent

but i'll still see you in my sleep

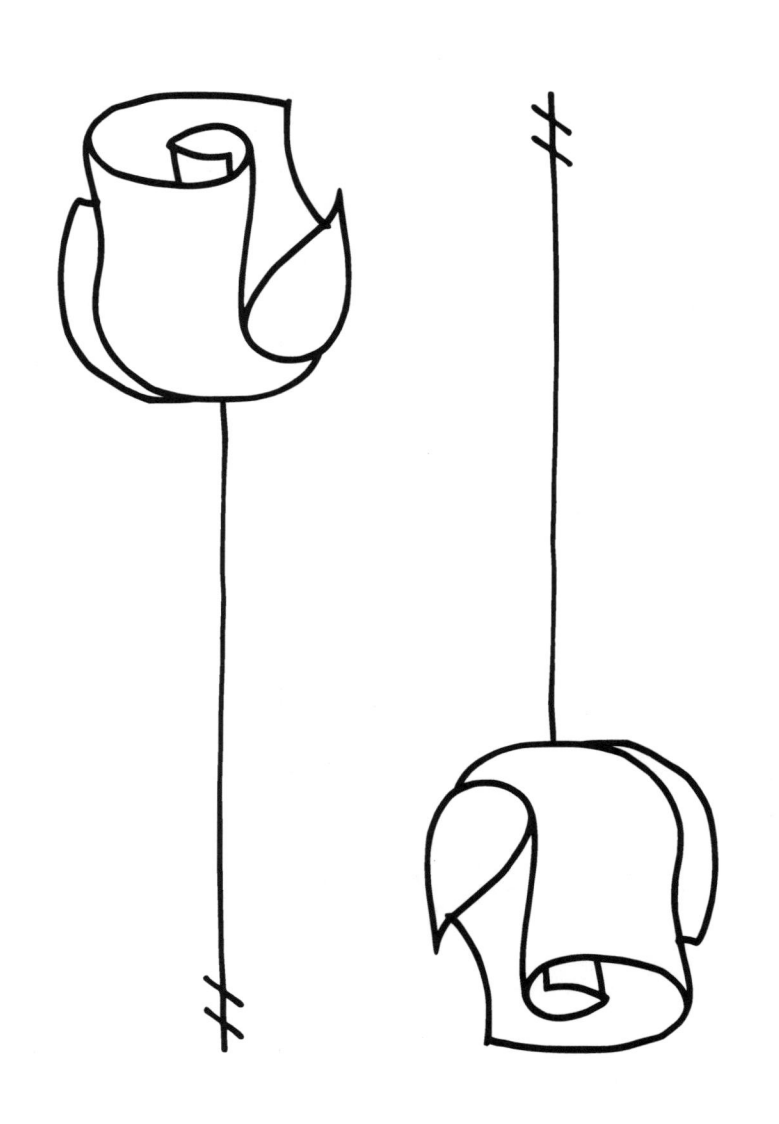

i don't always wear this smile
but i could never prove that's true

for you only see
the version of me

that's standing next to you

after every sunset

your clothes are on my floor

but i'm still waiting for a sunrise

where you don't head for the door

this shouldn't hurt so bad
because our time was only fleeting

but you cracked all of my ribs

with the way my heart was beating

⟶

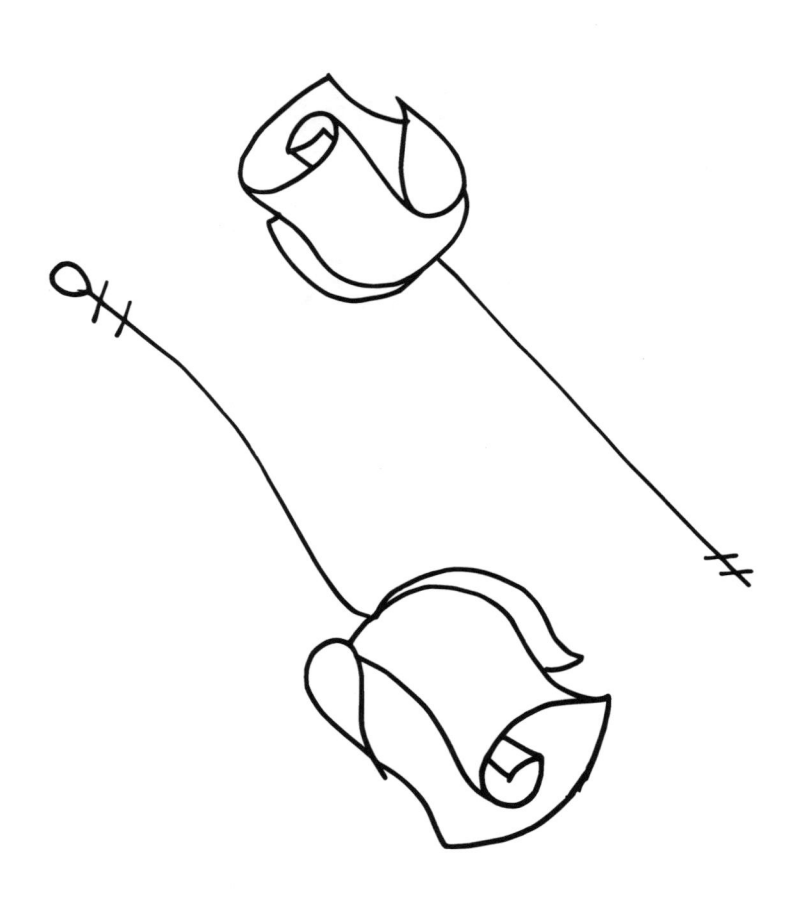

if this town feels too familiar

and you've memorized all the faces

there's some room here in my car

grab my hand and let's go places

i've learned how to move on

when you leave no other choice

but when the next girl says my name

i'll still hear it in your voice

→

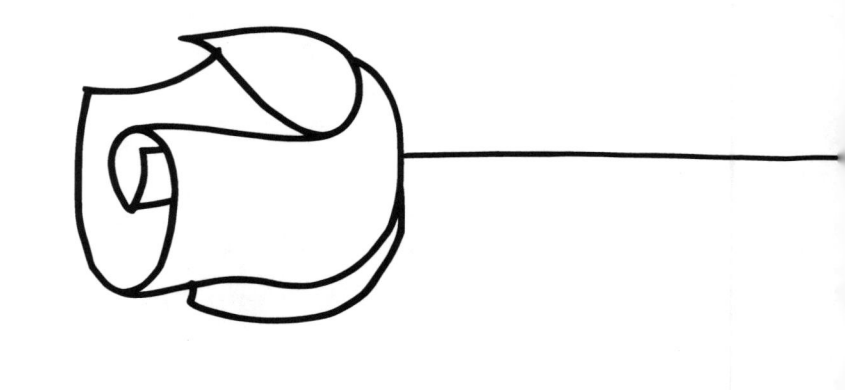

→

you're a worse addiction than cigarettes

every morning you don't stay

because it's not good for my lungs

to take my breath and walk away

i can hear the screams of words

you're keeping trapped behind your teeth

and i fear we'll just stay friends

because i can't get you to speak

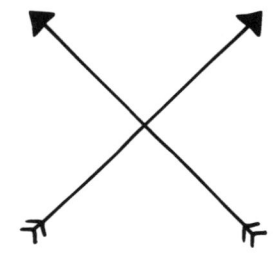

so i'll try to make you laugh

for when a smile parts your lips

all your words about desire

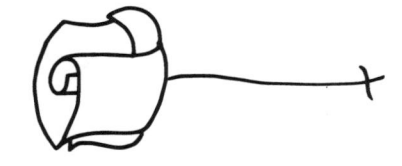

may get free and start to slip

⟶

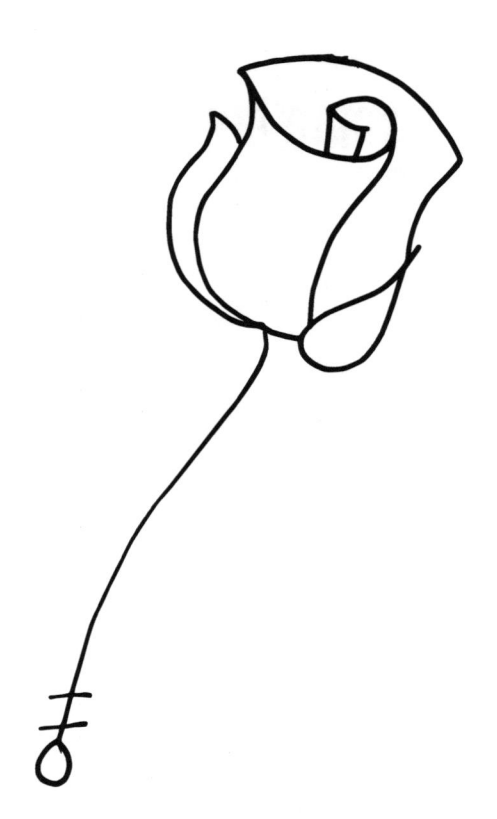

you can run back to my heart

but you're gonna have to knock

because you had the only key

and you made me change the lock

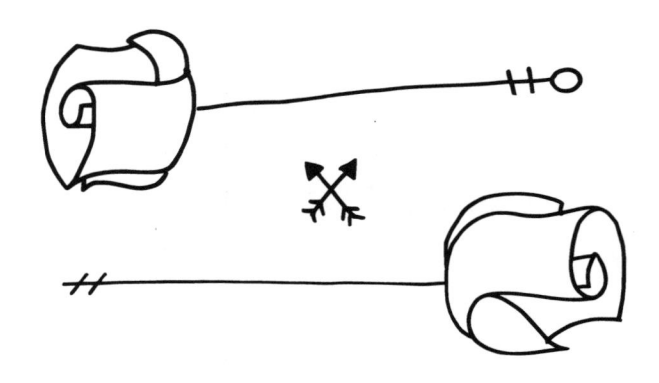

we've been cowards with our feelings

and the night's no longer young

so let's drink until desire

tears the words off both our tongues

→

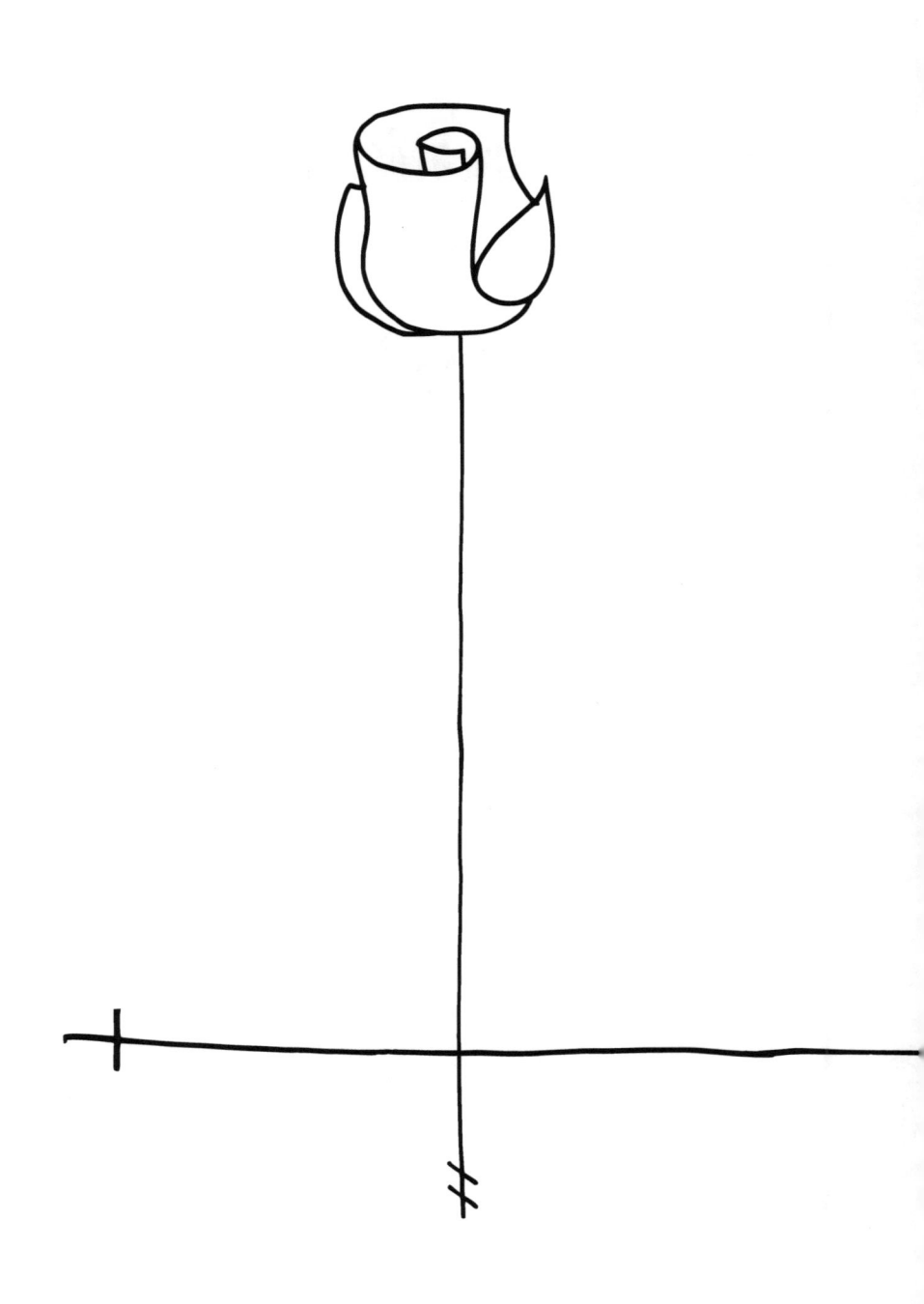

on the first day our eyes met

i went weak in both my knees

so let's sleep through stormy nights

because my legs can't take the breeze

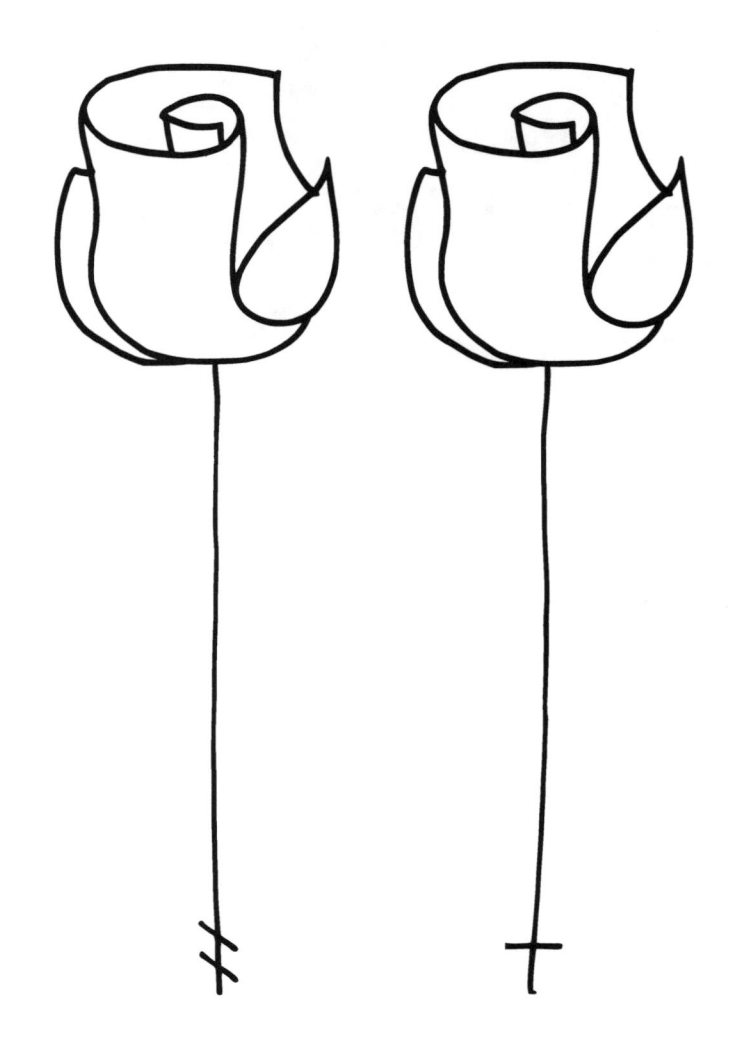

my friend's weren't all so lucky

to get parents like i had

but i think fondly of my youth

and that's because of you and dad

→

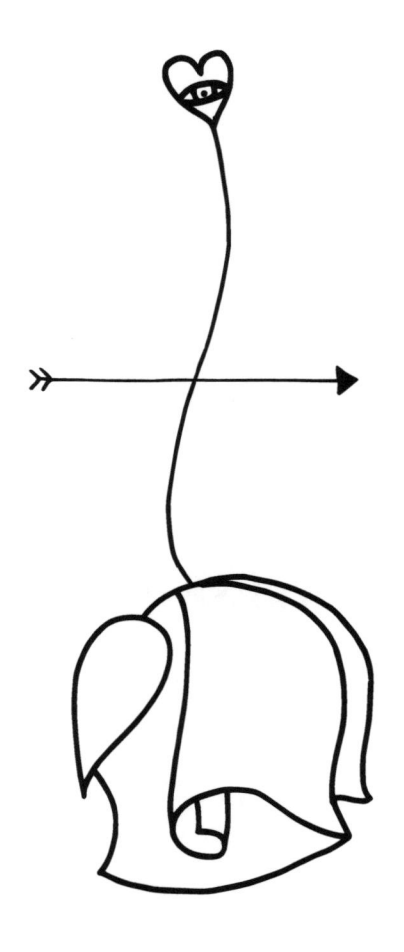

i've been calling you my dream girl
but i've learned that that's not true

because i never get to sleep

when all i do is think of you

i've been feeling sad at sunset
but i don't wonder why

because i'm missing the beauty who
lights up my life

after color abandons the sky

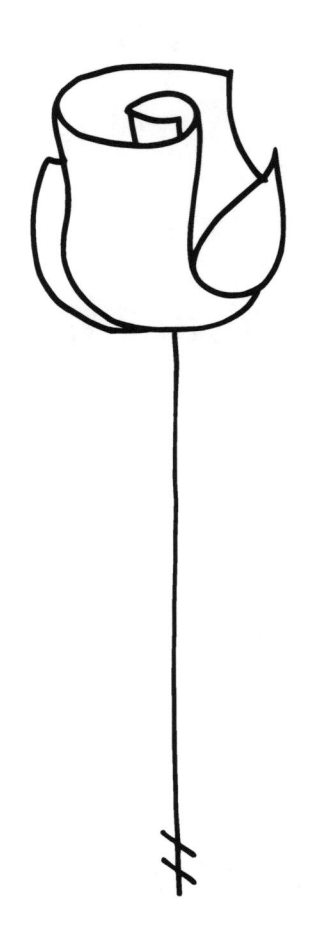

→

darlin' you can drive me wild

so let's take off down the street

and i swear i'll drive forever

if you're in my shotgun seat

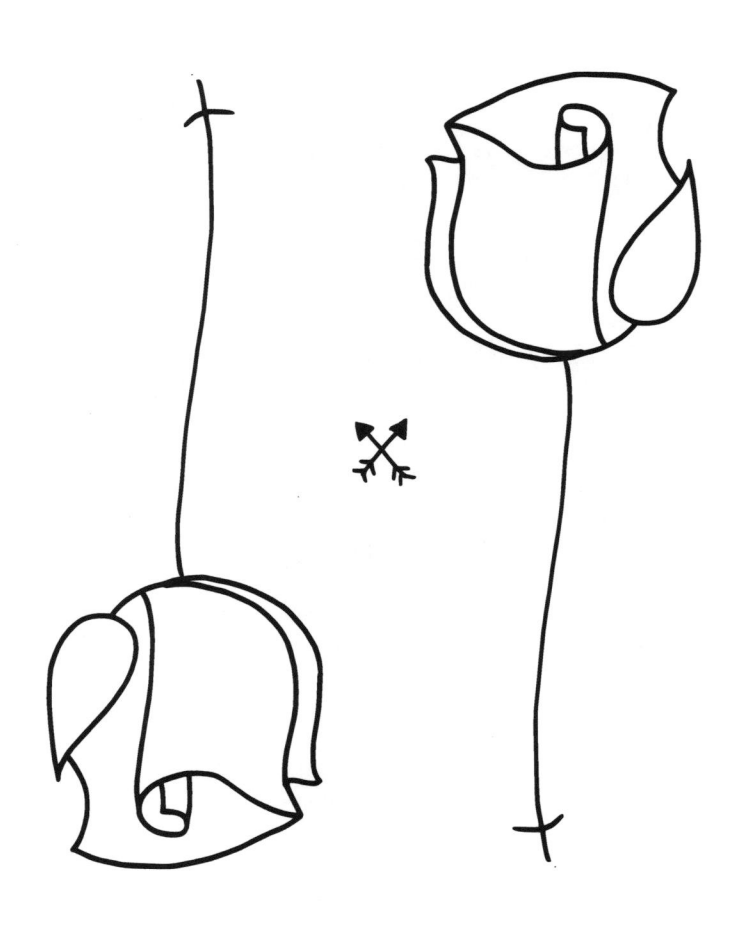

this city's full of people
that i'll probably never meet

because when you're so far away

all i see are empty streets

i'm jealous of the sunsets

for the way they catch your eye

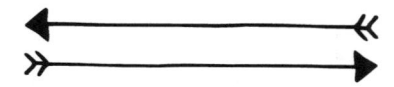

because i can't get your attention

there's no color in my sky

let's go sleeping on the beach

because there's beauty in the stars

and you'll see that constellations

look no different than your scars

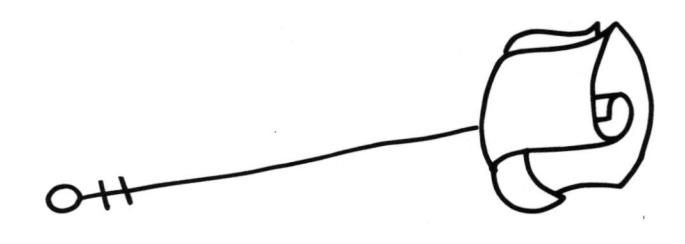

if you asked me where i'd travel
if i had the means to roam
i'd say if you're not coming with me
then i'd rather just stay home

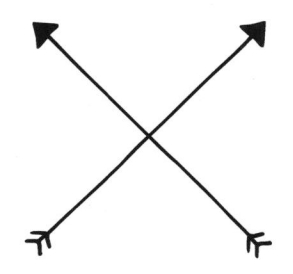

there's a hill down to the south
where your mom and i would go
to watch the sun go down

and the buildings start to glow
and we always thought it sad
the city's working late again

to afford a life as free
as she and i right then
well what they would never know

is we had pennies to our name
but we lived the richest lives
with two hearts we'd set aflame

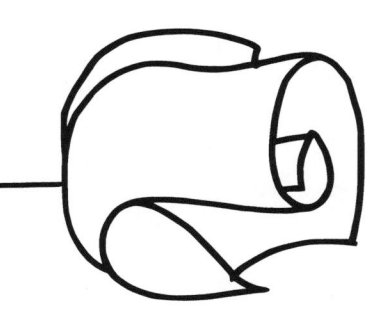

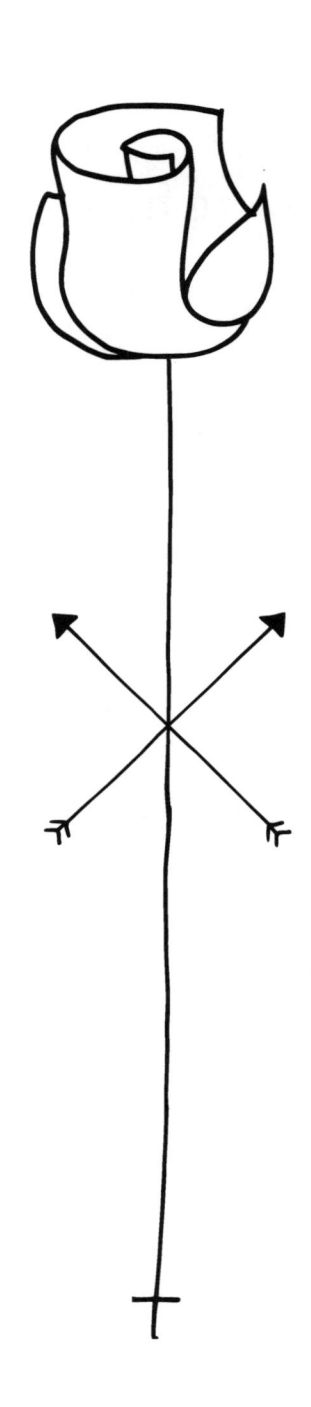

→

i've been writing these words to rip out your heart

but really they're just breaking mine

because in my life you're a grandiose verse

and in yours i'm no more than a line

i'm just passing through your town

so we know what morning brings

but there's summer in the air

and we're yearning for a fling

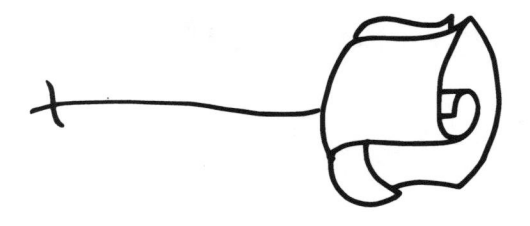

for it makes us feel alive

to get lost inside new eyes

and we live for perfect nights

that may lead to missing flights

⟶

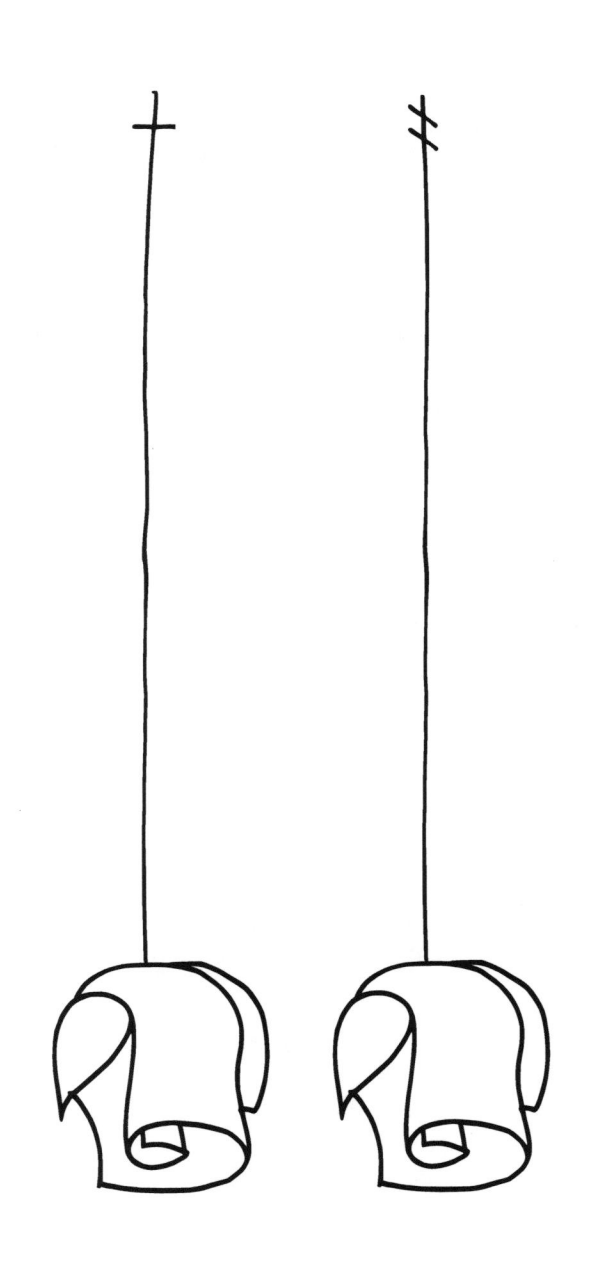

i made one hundred friends

to fill the void you left behind

but when it's time to fall asleep

you're the one that's on my mind

you've got a wild side
but you have no one to adore

and i've got an empty heart
that i need someone to explore

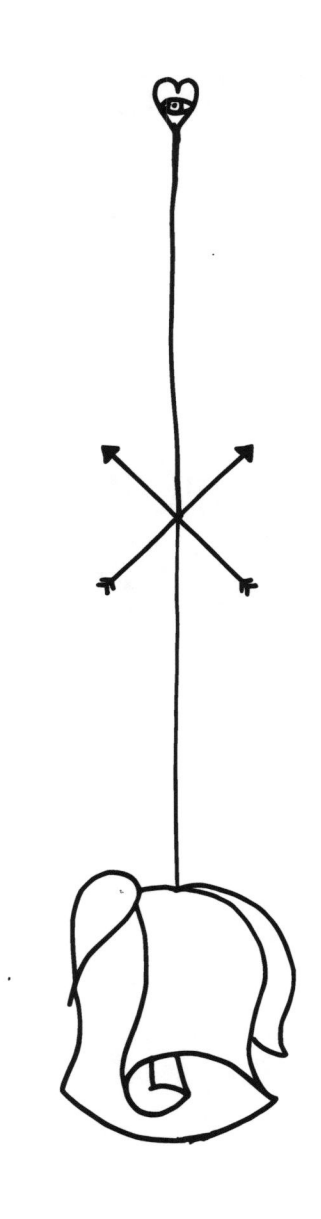

i can't seem to find the words

to tell you we're not meant to be

because you're absolutely perfect

you're just not perfect for me

⟶

we're halfway drunk in our old town

so darlin' raise a glass

because tomorrow you'll be gone

but tonight's about the past

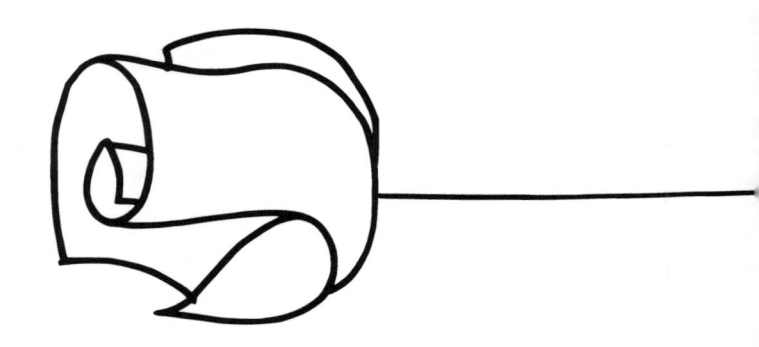

and we'll drink for all the years

that we wasted miles away

and if we drink enough tonight

i hope tomorrow you might stay

it's looking like we'll just stay friends

and truthfully that's fine

i just hope your smile makes his day

the way it has for mine

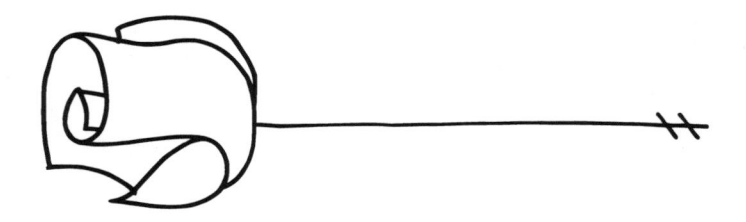

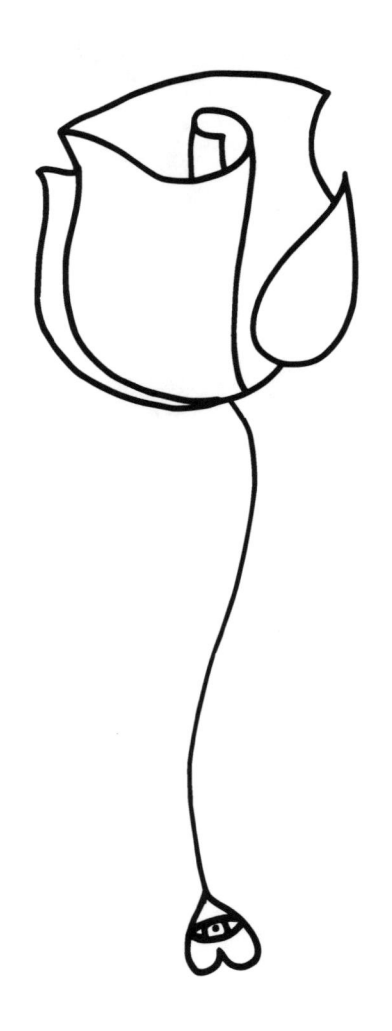

→

to prove to you i love you

i've devised a little test

when you smile in my direction

watch my heart beat out my chest

for six or seven months
we got lost inside a fling

and now you might be gone
but i wouldn't change a thing

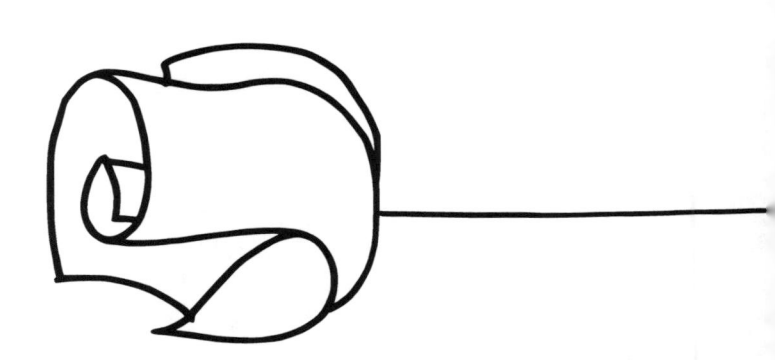

because i may forget your birthday
and the place we used to meet

but i won't forget the feeling
of my heart growing complete

i don't need to see the world

if i spend my life with you

because our home might not be pretty

but i'll have my favorite view

you swore you'd wait for love

until it swept you off your feet

≫———————▶

but then your friends walked down the aisle

and you didn't feel complete

now you wake up with a man

but you're sleeping with resentment

since you didn't fall in love

you just settled for contentment

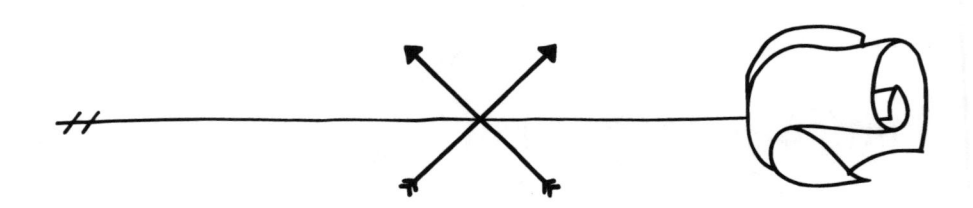

⟶

she'll toss and turn beside me

as you're running through my head

because i can't seem to forget you

and neither can my bed

she was the kind of girl i wish i'd met

after i lived enough to know

that you don't take love for granted

and you never let it go

⟶

i'm stuck inside on sunny days

when flowers are in bloom

because i'm trying to forget you

and they smell like your perfume

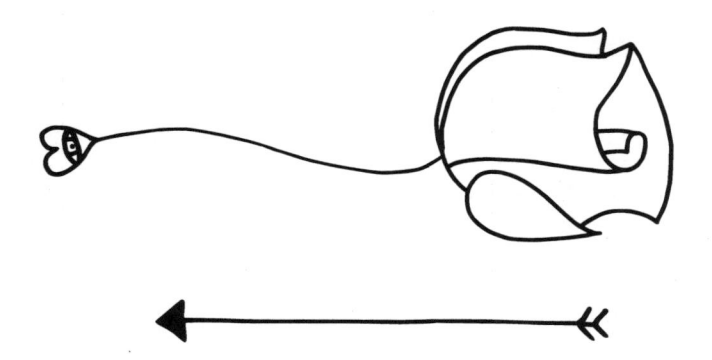

i remember being strangers

only seven months ago

staring as you poured my coffee

and then taking it to go

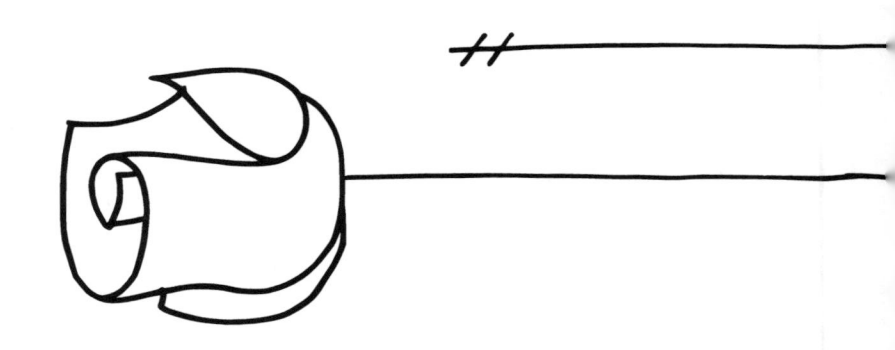

then one day i found some courage

shared the feelings in my head

now we still meet over coffee

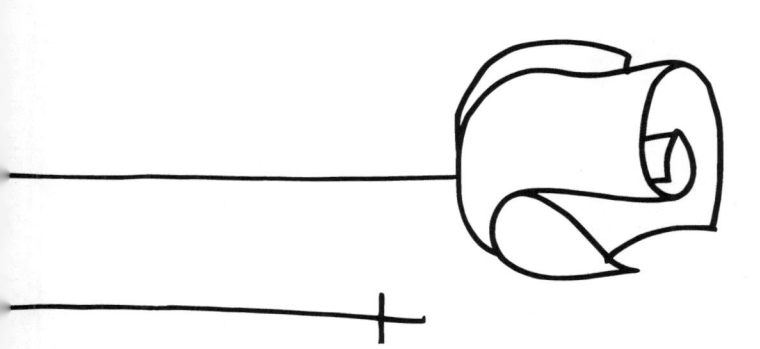

but we're drinking it in bed

a part of me will always be

at 4th & rio grande

where the glimmer in your eye

invited me to hold your hand

well our fingers split up months ago

and now we never speak

but our blood has stained the corner

where our beating hearts would leak

✖

write here.

spill it.
―――

let it out.
―――

what's on your mind?
———

destroy this page.

describe your first kiss.
———

write about her.
———

write about him.
———

#itdoesntrhymeandidontcare

tell me about the best night of your life.
———

Special thanks to everyone who supported me or encouraged me in my journey to get this book published:

My friends, especially @sandreckoner, Ben Hughes, @sean_hob, @jeysonpaez, @thevuvobandit and @jerr_e, @philipandersonedsel, @cheesim and @stephisdead.

All the great people at @Instagram, especially @jeffreydgerson.

My coworkers at Main Street Hub, especially @lwooding2, @ellep189, @robzie81, @bethwaldman, Chris Bendana, @driving_at_night and @pljohnson.

My friend & designer @mattthompson.

The folks at @BuzzFeed, most notably @conzpreti.

My family, especially my Uncle @kciamp for pushing me, my parents for still loving me after reading some of my poems (Thanks Mom!), and my sister, @maeci16, for always trying to stir up trouble by convincing them each one is autobiographical.

Last by not least, thanks to everyone who inspired me to write: the girls who shared my bed and kissed me like they meant it. The friends who got in my car late at night and would sing along to bad music as we sped down empty highways. The flings, the relationships, the nights we shared together. I've come to terms with the fact that these moments may start to become few and far between as we grow older and farther apart, but you can't take the memories from us and we'll always have these short poems to remind us of the ups and downs we experienced together over these past few years.

So, I'm signing off for book #1. Until we talk again, remember: you should feel more than you're supposed to.

So get out and do it.

About the author

Tony Ciampa is a dude that lives in Austin, TX via Boston, MA via Woolwich, ME via a few other places along the way. At the time of this writing, he's 22 years old. But soon he won't be anymore. That's just how life goes. If his college tuition hadn't been so damn high he might have given Northeastern University a shout out here to say thanks for teaching him a few things that enabled him to publish his first book. Maybe in 300 years when he's out of debt he'll reconsider. For now he'll just shout out Woolwich Central School. Go Wildcats. He does freelance copywriting and sometimes photography too. Probably going to be really rich and successful someday but it just hasn't happened yet. If you're ever in Austin, you might find him riding his bike through scenic neighborhoods at golden hour, lying on his couch watching @SportsCenter reruns and eating @capecodpotatochips, or writing at @thebrewandbrew.

His handle on Instagram and elsewhere is @emolabs.

It'd be chill if you followed him.

About the designer

Matt Thompson is a Designer living and working in Austin, TX via San Antonio, TX. Professionally, he is a Co-Founder of @sturdymfgco. Personally, he is 27 years old, a musician, photographer, thinker, do-er, maker of sorts and listener. If you're in Austin and happen to find him, he will most likely be riding his bike with some friends, playing with his dog Champ, lying on his couch watching baseball, hockey or professional wrestling, or working...usually working.

His handle on Instagram and most other places is @mattthompson give or take a few a's.

He would appreciate a follow.

Made in the USA
Middletown, DE
20 December 2014